The Real Jesus

WILLIAM BROCKER

THE REAL JESUS

Copyright 2017 by William Brocker

All rights reserved.

DEDICATION

Dedicated to my Lord Jesus and my girl Tovana,
the amazing wife he gave me.

TABLE OF CONTENTS

CHAPTER ONE

OUT OF RELIGION

I had been baptized a couple of times—once drunk (yes, you read that right) and once sober —but now I look back to my dismay and see that all I got was wet...

In 1984 at 19 years old, I went to work as a deputy district clerk in the Galveston County Courthouse in Galveston, Texas. Working there so closely with district court judges, prosecutors, defense attorneys, and the Sheriff's Department was truly awesome. I worked in and around that courthouse for a decade, watching and being a part of many exciting things. Over the years, I worked as a deputy district clerk and jury specialist, and later I owned a court services company where we did civil investigations, served subpoenas, modifications, and citations, and performed depositions on written questions; mostly collecting medical and bank records for cases and putting them together in a useful manner for the attorneys and courts to use for trial preparation. I sat in on hundreds of court cases during those years. I saw jury and bench trials, civil and criminal, and I witnessed and admired skilled attorneys and judges work their craft for years. Many of them were great friends of mine. I saw the law work perfectly as it was intended, I saw it abused, I saw people lose all they had, and I saw others gain great wealth. I saw the innocent and the guilty convicted and set free, I testified regarding things which brought me no pleasure. And I saw men sentenced to death.

This was certainly an exciting and seemingly prosperous time in my life, although I was not a Christian—I thought I was and would have told you so, but my faith wasn't real in any way that mattered to God. As mentioned, I had been baptized a couple of times—once drunk as a Methodist and once sober as Greek Orthodox—but trust me when I say I was not saved. Like so many in our culture, I put on airs of religiosity, but I had no true relationship with Jesus Christ, and I had certainly never yielded my life to him or his teachings. I was wild and reckless, but still managed to maintain some outer appearance of well-doing and professionalism. I thought I had it all together, but I was really just trying to fill the God-sized void in me through prodigal living and selfish pride.

Jesus told Nicodemus in the Gospel of John that if we are not born again, we will never see the kingdom of God.[1] I was truly born again on November 20, 2007. I got on my knees and, with tears running down my face, I pled with Jesus, "If you will come into my heart and my home today, I will never ask you to leave." It's maybe not the standard prayer of salvation we might offer someone to repeat after us, but I can tell you that it was effective. God is faithful: Jesus Christ did come and save me that day, and since that day I have never departed from my commitment to live for and honor him. I am eternally grateful for Christ's salvation.

The problem with coming to know the Lord after living wild and reckless (besides the potential for early death before salvation) is that the mind remains messed up, even after salvation. Our *spirit* is saved, renewed, and sealed,[2] but the part of us that we relate to is our soul. Our soul is the part of us that we are aware of and can discern with our natural senses. The soul consists of our mind, will, and emotions....our personality. These elements have been programmed with garbage like anger, bitterness, unforgiveness, self-centeredness, and all sorts of pain and disappointment. The biggest pieces of garbage I dealt with as a new believer were condemnation and unworthiness. All the bad

---

[1] Jesus answered and said unto him, Verily, verily, I say unto thee, except a man be born again, he cannot see the kingdom of God. (John 3:3 KJV)

[2] In whom ye also trusted, after that ye heard the word of truth, the gospel of your salvation: in whom also after that ye believed, ye were sealed with that holy Spirit of promise... (Ephesians 1:13 KJV)

behavior, bitterness, and rejection from my life before Christ haunted me, and I couldn't resolve how I was saved or loved— and this negative thinking was actually hindering God's great plan for my life. To help me with this, the Lord did a beautiful thing. He appeared to me in a dream. I was in a courtroom—a dirty, dimly lit courtroom. Standing there before the elevated judge's bench, I was the one on trial. Not only that, I knew I was guilty. I didn't know what crime I was charged with, but I knew I was guilty. I felt the same dread of garbage from my waking hours. A lifetime of shame and unworthiness weighed on my soul, and I knew I was in big trouble. Then I looked to my right, and my Lord Jesus was standing next to me. I gazed upon him, and my legs gave way. I fell to my knees in the presence of his glory, his beauty, and the love I felt in my heart from him and for him. Gathering myself, I remembered from my work in Galveston County that this type of legal proceeding always includes a prosecuting attorney, witnesses, and a judge. I searched the room, but none of these people were there—no one there to accuse me, no one to charge me, no one to judge me—just me and Jesus. I turned back to the Lord and gazed upon His face—the radiance, the quiet strength, the meekness, the thoughtfulness, the compassion, the splendor, the integrity, the love— and then I watched him turn and walk away. I reached out to him and begged to go with him, but he continued walking—straight through the wall. Then he was gone. I so badly wanted him to take me with him, and I began crying at being left behind. A voice from the back of the room spoke to me, that of another accused person. "He was looking at *you*! You are free!" I was free—guilty as could be, but free as a bird because of Jesus. And there was no one there to convict me or even bring a charge against me... because of Jesus.

You see, the Redeemer of the World had already overpaid the price for my sin and for yours. He was punished already, and God credits our lives with *Christ's* righteousness.[3,4,5,6] So though this world may hate you and though there may be consequences for your actions, from the moment you placed your trust in Jesus, God put away your sin and forgot all about it, giving you eternal life and enabling joy in your earthly life. Satan can no longer make accusations regarding you before God. He may tell you differently, but he is lying. Jesus is your advocate— the best attorney of all time—and he is on your side. He loves you very much, and having revelation knowledge of this love will help you conquer all the fears, discouragement, guilt, and doubts presented by this life. It will cause you to live holy as a byproduct

---

[3] Who shall bring any charge against God's elect? It is God who justifies. Who is to condemn? Christ Jesus is the one who died—more than that, who was raised—who is at the right hand of God, who indeed is interceding for us. (Romans 8:33–34 ESV)

[4] ...And if any man sin, we have an advocate with the Father, Jesus Christ the righteous... (1 John 2:1 KJV)

[5] But to him that worketh not, but believeth on him that justifieth the ungodly, his faith is counted for righteousness. (Romans 4:5 KJV)

[6] For there is one God, and one mediator between God and men, the man Christ Jesus; (1 Timothy 2:5 KJV)

of the relationship you have with him, out of love and gratitude. You will desire that your life not cause him pain or tarnish his reputation, and you will naturally disallow the open doors to the enemy that a sinful life presents because the life you now live is Jesus living in you and through you.[7]

The condition in which I lived, void of relationship with God, is representative of so many Christians today—believing Christ exists and is who he says he is, but not submitting to him or trusting him. God's people need to come out of this stagnancy and enter into real relationship to impact their lives and the lives of others. We need to get our minds off ourselves and onto Jesus. We need to allow him to really transform our hearts and minds[8]—and experience the fullness of the life he has for us.

---

[7] I have been crucified with Christ; it is no longer I who live, but Christ lives in me; and the *life* which I now live in the flesh I live by faith in the Son of God, who loved me and gave Himself for me. (Galatians 2:20 NKJV)

[8] I beseech you therefore, brethren, by the mercies of God, that ye present your bodies a living sacrifice, holy, acceptable unto God, which is your reasonable service. And be not conformed to this world: but be ye transformed by the renewing of your mind, that ye may prove what is that good, and acceptable, and perfect, will of God. (Romans 12:1–2 KJV)

CHAPTER TWO

GOD'S DESIGN FOR HIS PEOPLE

The Children of God

Imagine a king in a magnificent and glorious kingdom. In this kingdom are all the riches and treasures you could ever dream of. It is a land of peace. Everyone loves one another, and there is no lack. One day the king speaks to one of his children, whom he dearly loves. He tells the child that there is trouble in another land, a land far away, full of other people whom he loves as well. They are suffering terribly; drought, famine, poverty, sickness, and fear have taken hold of the land. These terrible problems have caused the people to do things they normally would not have done... and to lose hope. He asks his child to go to this land and help the people. He makes available everything at his disposal to use as a means to rectify the problems in that place. The child enthusiastically agrees to go help the people of the faraway land and heads out on the journey, bringing with him silver and gold, precious things, caravans of food supplies, fresh water, medicine, and valuable information from all the sharpest minds of the kingdom, information designed to teach the people of the land to understand the cause of their problems, as well as valuable information on how to solve them

Much time goes by, and the king hears nothing from his child. He waits for a very long time, but when he still receives no word, he sends others out looking. They go to the distant land, and when they arrive they find things to be worse than seemed possible. The people of the distant land are in serious trouble. The condition of the people is worse than they had heard about, and all the people are very sick. They have no money for food, no medicine for the sickness that runs rampant, and no one seems to have any hope or ideas for a brighter future.

To their surprise, those sent by the king come across all the resources sent with the child in an empty valley, seemingly abandoned. They then find the child of the king curled up in the corner of a hut in a village overrun with poverty, sickness, and despair. The child has become one of the land's people. The child is startled to have been found and begins to weep, asking why they have taken so long, why the king has done nothing, why the people have been left without even hope.

This story is our story. God is our Father, the King of all creation. Our home is in heaven with Him, but we are here as ambassadors of His love, His provision, His salvation. But somehow in the time we've been here, we have abandoned the supplies and information given to us for aid, we have forgotten our purpose for being in this faraway land, we haven't even taken care of ourselves. Instead, we have entrenched ourselves in the land. Physically and spiritually we have become sick and poor, and we tend to blame our Father in heaven.

A Perfect Creation By a Perfect Being

In the beginning God created the heavens and the earth. Now the earth was formless and empty, darkness was over the surface of the deep, and the Spirit of God was hovering over the waters.
Genesis 1:1–2 NIV

In the beginning was the Word, and the Word was with God, and the Word was God. He was with God in the beginning. Through him all things were made; without him nothing was made that has been made. In him was life, and that life was the light of all mankind. The light shines in the darkness, and the darkness has not overcome it.
John 1:1–5 NIV

Then God said, "Let us make mankind in our image, in our likeness..."
Genesis 1:26 NIV

We have heard many times that in the beginning God created the heavens and the earth and all living beings. To unpack this statement, we must first acknowledge that the statement is limited by our human structure of time: God always was, always is, and always will be. His time and existence are boundless, without beginning and without end. I always say it like this: God created time, but He is not in it. He allowed it to play out in His mind completely. That's why He knows the end from the beginning. This helps people understand that while God is all-powerful and all-knowing, He never interferes with the free will of mankind. This makes the miracle of salvation all the more magnificent.

Second, we must understand that God is a triune being—Father (God), Son (Jesus/God), and Holy Ghost (Spirit/God). In explaining the Holy Trinity, a triangle is often drawn, with each point representing a member of the Godhead:

A triangle's lines, though, have endpoints, and one or more points on the triangle always lie above or below another point or points, making it a poor choice for understanding the Holy Trinity. It is more accurate (in humbly attempting to visually represent the Trinity) to use a circle, which better symbolizes the never-ending oneness of Father-Son-Spirit:

Incredibly, this holy being created life and everything we know to reveal Himself to us. He—who is unseen and uncreated—revealed Himself to and for us—natural, carnal, created beings—through things that can be seen—His creation. God's creation, including humanity, was made perfect in the likeness of Himself.

The Bad News

When the woman saw that the fruit of the tree was good for food and pleasing to the eye, and also desirable for gaining wisdom, she took some and ate it. She also gave some to her husband, who was with her, and he ate it. Then the eyes of both of them were opened, and they realized they were naked; so they sewed fig leaves together and made coverings for themselves.
Genesis 3:6–7 NIV

...for all have sinned and fall short of the glory of God...
Romans 3:23 NIV

Another story we've heard many times is that of Adam and Eve in the Garden of Eden: God created man and woman and placed them in a garden to live with Him and have all of their needs met. A serpent (the Evil One) deceived Eve into eating fruit from a forbidden tree; she in turn gave some to Adam who was with her. Eating the forbidden fruit gave them knowledge of evil that God did not intend for them to have. God banished Adam and Eve from the garden because of their disobedience.

This is most simply the story of sin entering God's perfect creation, corrupting it, poisoning it, and bringing enmity between us and God. Because sin entered creation, everyone born from Adam's seed—meaning you and me and everyone we know—is a sinner. Since Adam, everyone ever born of man has been born with a sin-nature, and there's nothing we can do on our own to escape it, make up for it, or eliminate it from our lives. No matter how hard we work, how much good we do, or how nice we are to people, we have been separated from God by sin, more specifically, the sin-nature we inherited from Adam. This is the bad news.

The Good News

For God so loved the world that he gave his one and only Son, that whoever believes in him shall not perish but have eternal life.
John 3:16 NIV

For it is by grace you have been saved, through faith—and this is not from yourselves, it is the gift of God.
Ephesians 2:8 NIV

To reconcile the fallen world to Himself, God the Father—in His mercy and because He loves us so much—sent His Son Jesus Christ to our world in human form to redeem us, to restore us, to heal us. Our Savior Jesus Christ is the second person of the Holy Trinity. He was born of a virgin and walked among us in human form... fully man, yet fully God. Christ's human birth is critical, as is his paternity—he is the Son of God, not a son of Adam, meaning he was born without the sin-nature passed down from Adam, unlike us. Being physically born of a woman, however, makes Christ legally our kinsman redeemer. It was man who forfeited our relationship with God by yielding to the devil, so it had to be man to get it back. Christ lived a sinless life, took our place on the cross, bearing our sin, rejection, illnesses, disease, poverty, and everything else that came from the curse of sin and death. He laid down his life, was buried, and on the third day was resurrected from the dead, which became the ultimate defeat of sin. Christ ascended and now sits at the right hand of God in heaven, serving forever as our High Priest, interceding to God on our behalf. Now, by simply placing our trust in Christ and asking him to be Lord of our life, God imputes his righteousness unto us. When we believe and confess Christ as Lord, that old sin-nature is done away with forever. God renews our spirit, making it perfect and holy, and then seals it with the promised Holy Spirit as a guarantee of the eternal life we have entered into with Him. The cross of Jesus Christ effectively becomes our bridge back to the God we were separated from. This is the good news.

The redemption that we receive through Jesus Christ is a free gift from God and is a testament to how much He loves you and me—He loves us and sent us a Savior, even in our weak and helpless state, while we were yet sinners. And just as God created the world and everything we know in order to point to His glory, He likewise requires all the glory for salvation—so He does all the work. We are therefore saved by grace alone through faith alone. There is nothing we can do to earn salvation and it does not come as a reward, so in no way can we boast. No one can ever enter heaven and say it was by their own doing—it happens through Christ alone. This grace is available to everyone, but forced upon no one, further proving God's love for His children in giving them free will.

The Grace-Filled Number Five

As described, there are five basic elements of our faith:

1. Father
2. Son
3. Spirit

These first three elements make up the Trinity. The number one means unity, and the number two means division (or simply implies that there is another). The third element joins the first two together to make them one again, creating divine perfection. As one being, the Holy Trinity created, pointing to the final two elements:

4. Creation
5. Grace

The final and fifth element, grace, is defined as a disposition to be generous or helpful, mercy, clemency, or a favor rendered by one who need not do so. Coming from God, grace is the unearned, unmerited, and undeserved blessing and favor of our Father, Creator, and Savior. Grace is revealed time and time again in God's Word, marked by the number five. The Bible includes many numbers, each with a specific meaning, and the number five is no different. When we see this number in the Bible, God is generally pointing to His amazing grace:

- When Abram and Sarai were shown favor by God and called upon Him, He added the fifth letter of the Hebrew alphabet, h (hey), to their names, making them Abraham and Sarah.[9]

- Deuteronomy, the fifth book of the Bible, tells the story of God taking care of His people, not because of their goodness, but because He chose them and loved them.

- In Genesis, Joseph told Benjamin, "God be gracious to you, my son."[10] During a later meal, Benjamin's serving was five times as much as the others. Then again later, Benjamin was given five changes of clothes.[11] (In this story, Joseph and Benjamin are type and shadow of Jesus Christ and the Church—you.)

- When David fought Goliath, he chose five smooth stones and took him down by the power of God alone.[12]

- When Jesus was approached by Satan in the wilderness, he quoted the book of Deuteronomy, the fifth book of the Torah, in every response to his enemy, easily

---

[9] Genesis 17
[10] Genesis 43:29 NIV
[11] Genesis 45:22
[12] 1 Samuel 17

defeating him with the Word of God alone.[13]

- Jesus turned five loaves of bread into 5,000 to feed people who were hungry.[14]

- The fifth Psalm tells us how God surrounds us with His favor (grace) as a shield.

- The fifth book of the New Testament, Acts, tells of the amazing Acts of the Apostles who had recently scattered and even denied the Lord when trouble came. But given God's amazing grace and the power of the Holy Spirit, they performed many miracles and established the church.

- The Israelites made five main offerings, which would eventually be replaced by the ultimate offering of Christ on the cross because of God's love for His children.

In the Bible, God's love letter to His children, God has made no mistakes and has done nothing by accident. The number five points to grace—the grace that God desires for us to accept as His gift through Jesus Christ. [15]

---

[13] Matthew 4, Luke 4

[14] Matthew 14, Mark 6, Luke 9, John 6

[15] God has marked my own life with many fives as well—born the youngest of five children on the fifth day of the fifth month of the sixty-fifth year. My personal belief is that God knew it would take such a powerful repetition for me to believe He could actually love and forgive someone like me. He did, and He does. Thanks be to God.

Our Assignment

> *...I no longer live, but Christ lives in me.*
> *Galatians 2:20 NIV*

> *All this is from God, who reconciled us to himself*
> *through Christ and gave us the ministry of*
> *reconciliation.*
> *2 Corinthians 5:18 NIV*

Many Christians understand life here on earth as something to be endured until that day when we finally see Jesus and are completely transformed into his image in the twinkling of an eye. This understanding majorly misses what God wants for you and for me. Yes, on that day we will know fully the things which we do not know now, and yes, we will put off the body of flesh for an eternal one, but God wants much more from us while we are here. He has a job for us to do, and He wants us to experience His fullness while we're here.

We are ambassadors, peculiar to this world, set apart by and sent by a loving Father, King, and God of all creation to administer help to the lost, sick, and dying people in this faraway land. In Christ, through the Holy Spirit, our Father has given us everything we need to help others and ourselves. Living inside us is the very power that raised Christ from the dead. Once we believe and accept redemption and salvation from Christ, we have the very mind and character of Christ in our born-again spirit; he has anticipated every need we will ever have and provided everything we will need in this life: We actually have Jesus' very own peace given to us as a gift on the last night of his life on earth. The perfect love of our Father is ours in abundance, and the joy of the Lord is our strength. Praise be to God for His unspeakable gift.

This is the work for which we were chosen, sent, and given authority to perform: We are to strengthen the weak by administering the baptism of the Holy Spirit. We are to heal them who are physically sick. We are to bind up the injured by administering inner healing of their emotional wounds and deliverance to those oppressed by the devil. We are to evangelize, seeking the lost and bringing back those who have strayed away from God. We are instructed and empowered to prophesy and speak life into any situation that does not line up with the Word of God. We are to deny any place for poverty, sickness, disease, depression, strife, divorce, anger, bitterness, unforgiveness, rebellion, and any other ungodly spirit or aspect of the curse of sin that rears its head. We are to disciple others and to be discipled ourselves, enjoying and exploring the measure and gifts of our brothers and sisters in Christ. We are to submit to one another in love. We are to reconcile people to God.

God desires so much for us and for those we meet while we are in this land,[16] yet somehow we have left all of our provisions in the valleys of our lives; we have neglected to apply (or really even seek to obtain) the provisions God has given us by grace through the sacrifice of His precious Son Jesus. The writer of Hebrews asks a pertinent question in this context—*How shall we escape if we neglect such a great salvation?*[17] If God has provided for everything we will ever need in this life, as well as the next, how is it that we suffer so in this life, never experiencing the fullness of what Jesus provided through the atonement of the cross?

---

[16] ...ye shall pass before your brethren armed, all the mighty men of valour, and help them; Until the LORD have given your brethren rest, as he hath given you, and they also have possessed the land which the LORD your God giveth them: then ye shall return unto the land of your possession, and enjoy it... (Joshua 1:14–15 KJV)

[17] Hebrews 2:3

CHAPTER THREE

MEANINGLESS GOOD

In the weeks following my salvation, I had very high expectations of what my life should look like. I wanted God to undo all the negative things in my life that I had brought upon myself. I had been saved for real, truly redeemed, and was changing and growing in my new relationship with God. I was getting a glimpse of God's ways from the Bible, and I wanted just that for me and my family. Because I had accepted the free gift of salvation, I wanted all the benefits of it to be manifest instantaneously. As far as I could tell, though, God was taking His time about it—after all, it had been approximately five weeks. My assumption, of course, was that He didn't love me and that I was somehow special in the sense that His goodness might be available to some, but I was just a reject. This wrong thinking is typical of so many believers—the impression that God's goodness toward us is based upon our actions, our behavior, our goodness instead of those qualities of Jesus.

At about this point in my faith, I found myself sitting in my truck in a Home Depot parking lot in the middle of the day, depressed, overwhelmed, full of grief and self-pity. In a moment, I was overwhelmed with an urgent need to pray. I didn't know what to pray, but I definitely knew I needed to. The Bible had told me that praying in the Spirit would build me up in my most holy faith and keep me in the love of God[18] and that the Spirit would intercede for me when I don't know what to pray.[19] I needed to get past my flesh and go right to the throne of God. So, I began very simply—I thanked God for saving me and told Him I needed Him. I said that I was seeking Him and was confused and felt all alone. Then, I began to pray in the Spirit—beautiful words uncommon and unknown to me. I began to weep, tears flowing like a fountain as I continued to pray louder and louder in the cab of the truck—the Holy Spirit was crying out to God.

In the Bible, the Apostle Paul speaks of praying in tongues more than anyone.[20] In fact, he thanked God for it and wished for us all to speak in tongues.[21] I didn't know what I was saying, but I knew it was all there—all the pain, all the doubt and confusion, all the pleading and longing for God's help was being

---

[18] Jude 1:20–21
[19] Romans 8:26
[20] 1 Corinthians 14:18
[21] 1 Corinthians 14:5

expressed through my spirit.[22] I was like a frightened child complaining to his father and pleading to get his way and for the father to make it all better. My prayer went on for what seemed to be five minutes or so; then I stopped because I had heard Him. In an audible voice as plain as day, I heard Jesus laughing. Not in a negative way—but in a loving and comforting way, like that father who laughs when comforting his child afraid of something that only the father knew there was no need to fear. No need because the father was there the whole time, protecting and covering, never for a moment willing to allow any harm to befall his child. That day in my truck, Jesus laughed and then He spoke, "You are my child whom I love... I am well pleased."[23]

My heartbreak turned to wholeness, my depression to happiness; my sobbing was now an expression of overwhelming joy at what I had just experienced. I knew God loved me and everything was okay. God is so good and He does love me, and you. But we should not be dependent upon Him speaking to us audibly, or giving us a visible sign or a goose bump. We need to nurture and develop our relationship with Him and place our trust in His Word so that we are always confident of His love. The best way to determine your value to God is by looking at the price He paid for you. Your Father in heaven gave all that He had when He gave His Son Jesus Christ to die for your sins on the cross. He

---

[22] 1 Corinthians 2:14
[23] Matthew 3:17

overpaid to redeem you, and the Word says He was pleased to do it.

Salvation Isn't About Good Behavior

...I came that they may have life, and have it abundantly.
Jesus Christ, John 10:10 NRSV

The Spirit alone gives eternal life. Human effort accomplishes nothing...
John 6:63 NLT

If hearing parts of my testimony and reading Jesus' powerful words from the Gospel of John about the abundant life Jesus came to provide us with excites you, perhaps you are where so many have been—tired of struggling and being burdened down by junk, by the situations and circumstances of this life, tired of strife, tired of the internal void, *craving peace and fulfillment.* Whether you're a believer or not, the Good News in this restless life is the same: Jesus Christ has made a way for us to find peace and fulfillment in knowing him. The internal void we sense and the fruitless search for things to fill it is really a longing for the One who created us, our need for God. Our need to be loved, cared for, and encouraged can only truly be found in relationship with the source of all love, our Father in heaven. As long as we try to fill this void through the things of the world or human relationships, we will always live disappointed. Whomever and wherever you are, *relationship* with Christ is the key.[24]

We as believers tend to create a god of our imagination—one who accepts us based upon the good we have done, not based on relationship. We attempt to justify those beliefs by comparing ourselves with the world around us. The problem with this logic is that the world is fallen and makes for poor comparison. God instructs us instead to compare ourselves to Him alone by looking into the righteous mirror of His Word, specifically by looking at the life and ministry of Jesus Christ.

If the concept of trusting in relationship with a savior for peace instead of creating it yourself makes you uncomfortable, congratulations—you're human. It's not easy to accept that all our good works earn us no special treatment with God (although living holy does have many wonderful benefits, see Chapter 6, Spiritual Garden). After all, the world in which we live works just that way—behave well, get good results; behave poorly, get bad results. God is not of this world, though, His ways are better than our ways, so we must work to accept His way of providing for us by the grace established through the cross of Jesus Christ, and using faith as the hand that takes of this provision from God. We must learn to stop listening to our fleshy minds and, instead, surrender to the mind of Christ.

When we understand that God's standard for our attitudes, relationships, and even thoughts is

---

[24] And this is eternal life, that they know you the only true God, and Jesus Christ whom you have sent. (John 17:3 ESV)

total perfection, our need for a savior becomes obvious. Our options are either to be perfect and rely upon that perfection to hold up under God's holy scrutiny—or to believe in and rely upon a savior who is perfect where we are not. This savior's work is completed. He has already provided forgiveness for every sin we have ever committed or ever will commit. He has provided healing for every sickness and disease that we will ever encounter. He has anticipated every single need we will ever have: spiritual, physical, financial, emotional, and relational. He loves us and desires for us to call upon him to be our Lord and Savior. He wants us to know him and to be known by him. He wants to teach us, through his Word, to come into agreement and cooperate with him. It is only then, by the power of the Holy Spirit living in us, that we will be able to live the abundant life that he intends us to have and has already provided for us.

It took me a long time and many loving and encouraging moments with the Lord like that day at Home Depot to understand that the life of loving and giving and well-doing that I am called to experience and live comes as a *byproduct* of my relationship with God, not as a means to obtain it. In other words, holiness, or agape[25] love, is the fruit and not the root of our relationship with our loving Father and His Son Jesus, and the power to live that life comes from the Holy Spirit, the third person of the Trinity, who

---

[25] One of the three Greek words for love; this one specific only to unending, unconditional love God has for His creation.

leads us through this life as we seek and submit to God.

In seeking the abundant life promised to us in John 10, one of our greatest needs—and hardest thing for us to do—is to rest in Jesus' finished work, to come *out of religion* and its human flaws of self-effort and tradition to save us, and *into relationship* with God through His Son, Jesus Christ. This is the entire reason we were created.

It's About Relationship

> *If we say we have fellowship with him while we walk in darkness, we lie and do not practice the truth. But if we walk in the light, as he is in the light, we have fellowship with one another, and the blood of Jesus his Son cleanses us from all sin.*
> *1 John 1:6–7 ESV*

> *And when Jesus was baptized, immediately he went up from the water, and behold, the heavens were opened to him, and he saw the Spirit of God descending like a dove and coming to rest on him;*
> *Matthew 3:16 ESV*

> *...and laying his hands on him he said, "Brother Saul, the Lord Jesus who appeared to you on the road by which you came has sent me so that you may regain your sight and be filled with the Holy Spirit." And immediately something like scales fell from his eyes, and he regained his sight. Then he rose and was baptized;*
> *Acts 9:17–18 ESV*

*...for John baptized with water, but you will be
baptized with the Holy Spirit...*
Jesus Christ, Acts 1:5 ESV

*Yes, what joy for those whose record the Lord has
cleared of guilt, whose lives are lived in complete
honesty!*
Psalm 32:2 NLT

So take a close look at whether you *really know* Christ. Most believers will gladly claim Jesus Christ as their Savior. That's an easy one. But when it comes to *submission* to Jesus, when it comes to "fellowship with God" and "practicing the truth" as said in 1 John, we then reject him as our Lord. This does not work, though—it's like saying, "The forgiveness part sounds good, but I can't let him tell me what to do; it's my life." To say we know God and continue living for ourselves is hypocrisy that God will eventually root out, expose, and judge. The goal here is to challenge us to call upon God for some real answers regarding our relationship with Him—to allow His light to shine into the dark places of our souls and allow His Word to tear down any religious mindsets that cause us to judge anything other than our own personal relationship with the One many of us already call our Lord.

Another critical element to consider when taking a hard look at your relationship with Christ is baptism. So many are baptized with water but never with the Holy Spirit. My own walk with God, in fact, began with a need to be baptized with the Holy Spirit, even though I had already been baptized with water. So, in a Denny's parking lot with the patient help of two ministers (and even though it was something I said I'd never do), I was baptized with the Holy Ghost, after which point I truly entered a more vibrant and powerful relationship with Jesus and the Father. Without the baptism in the Holy Spirit, I have come to see and believe that we will never walk in the power and victory Christ died to provide us with, and we will never truly fulfill all that God has for us in this life. According to Holy Scripture, these two types of baptism are different (although they can be performed together). Indeed, at Jesus' own baptism, Matthew tells us that he was baptized by water *and then by the Spirit of God*. It is only after this point that he begins his ministry—there is no history of Jesus ever performing a single miracle or healing act until *after* he was baptized with the Holy Ghost. Likewise, as described in Acts 9, Saul was first filled with the Holy Spirit and was then baptized by water, after which he was renamed Paul and was sent forth to become an apostle of Jesus Christ, healing people, bringing people to Christ, and is given credit for penning 13 of the New Testament books we rely on today. And in two examples perhaps most relevant to us, (1) the Apostle Paul makes it clear to new disciples in Christ that they need baptism by not just water, but by the Holy Spirit, and (2) Jesus Christ tells his disciples not to even try ministering to the world (even after they had been with him for more than three years) until they had been endued with power from on high:

> *And it happened that while Apollos was at Corinth, Paul passed through the inland country and came to Ephesus. There he found some disciples. And he said to them, "Did you receive the Holy Spirit when you believed?" And they said, "No, we have not even heard that there is a Holy Spirit." And he said, "Into what then were you baptized?" They said, "Into John's baptism." And Paul said, "John baptized with the baptism of repentance, telling the people to believe in the one who was to come after him, that is, Jesus." On hearing this, they were baptized in the name of the Lord Jesus. And when Paul had laid his hands on them, the Holy Spirit came on them, and they began speaking in tongues and prophesying.*
> *Acts 19:1–6 ESV*

> *And behold, I am sending the promise of my Father upon you. But stay in the city until you are clothed from on high.*
> *Jesus Christ, Luke 24:49 ESV*

If you find yourself dipping your feet in the water, unable to plunge into relationship with Christ and allow him to take over, especially if you have not been baptized in the Holy Spirit, this is the point where your abundant life gets lost. Perhaps you think you'll end up giving more than you receive. Perhaps you think you'll have to work too hard. Or sacrifice too much. Or suffer within God's will. Or maybe you just believe that God won't do as good a job as you will. Again, you're human and this is the natural human state. But I hope you will believe me when I tell you that God wants to take your natural and make it supernatural. The Christian life is impossible to live in our own strength. We need everything that God has for us, not only to be empowered to do all that He has for us to do, but in order to relate to and fellowship with our God and savior who loves us. Begin by being honest with God about your fears and lack of trust. He already knows everything about us inside and out; He can be hurt by us, but not deceived. By simply being open and honest with Him, and according to Psalm 32, we can step into total forgiveness and blessing. What an opportunity to enter or deepen relationship with our Creator and Savior, who wants to bless us more than we can fathom receiving.

CHAPTER FOUR

CHANGING FROM OLD TO NEW

God's Covenants

Whenever I bring clouds over the earth and the rainbow appears in the clouds, I will remember my covenant between me and you and all living creatures of every kind. Never again will the waters become a flood to destroy all life.
God, Genesis 9:14–15 NIV

I will establish my covenant as an everlasting covenant between me and you and your descendants after you for the generations to come, to be your God and the God of your descendants after you.
God, Genesis 17:7 NIV

> *This cup is the new covenant in my blood, which is*
> *poured out for you...*
> *Jesus Christ, Luke 22:20 NIV*

To understand how we are to have a real, meaningful relationship with Christ, we first need to understand where our relationship with God began. A quick way to do that is to look at covenants God has made with His people:

- In Genesis, humanity had disappointed its Creator with persistent and pervasive sin, so He wiped it out with a flood that covered the earth. God saved Noah and his family from the flood, promising them that He would never deal with His creation in that manner again. The rainbow is the beautiful sign of that promise—it represents God's compassion, mercy, protection, and love for His people.

- A few generations later, God made another covenant with His people through Abram. He promised that Abram would be the father of nations and kings, that his descendants would possess the land of Canaan, and that He would be their God. To seal the covenant, God changed Abram's name to Abraham, and as sign of the covenant, all male descendants were circumcised, marking them as belonging to God.

- When Christ came, died, and was resurrected, we received a new covenant—

the covenant of Christ taking our place on the cross and restoring us in righteousness to God. The signs of this covenant are Christ's body and Christ's blood, of which we partake symbolically through communion.

What the Covenants Mean Today

I am the vine, you are the branches: He that abides in me, and I in him, the same brings forth much fruit: for without me you can do nothing...
Jesus Christ, John 15:5 KJ2000
I can do all things through Christ who strengthens me.
Philippians 4:13 KJ2000

For I know the plans I have for you," declares the Lord, "plans to prosper you and not to harm you, plans to give you hope and a future. Then you will call on me and come and pray to me, and I will listen to you. You will seek me and find me when you seek me with all your heart..."
Jeremiah 29:11–13 NIV

Not long after I was saved, I had a wonderful encounter with God. Jesus had saved me and I was glad of it, but my heart was broken by all the wreckage of my past. I was continually in the Word and hungry for God. One day I stopped to put gas in my car, and while I was standing at the pump I was overwhelmed with grief, sorrow, and a longing for

God. I remember looking into the sun. It was beautiful as it set that evening... and though He seemed very distant from my heart, somehow at that moment, I knew that I had an audience with our Creator. Looking into that sunset, with tears streaming down my face, I cried out, "Lord I'm Seeking You!"

At that very moment, as if someone tapped me on the shoulder, I turned around. As I turned, I was completely enveloped by the most beautiful rainbow I have ever seen. It was right there...as if God himself had taken His brush and painted it over my head as I looked toward the sun and cried out to Him. It touched the ground on both sides, and at that moment I felt as if I were getting a glimpse into heaven. The tears began to flow even more as I was keenly aware of God's love and presence. I knew that rainbow had been placed there just for me, as a loving response to a child with a broken and contrite heart, from a caring Father. I didn't know all the spiritual ramifications of it at the time, but somehow I knew it meant I was protected. It meant He was there and He cared for me enough to show me a beautiful sign of His protection...and love.

The covenants are just as relevant and powerful for us as Christians today, and they all point to us needing to deepen our relationship with Christ. In the case of the Noahic covenant, God still desperately wants us to know that He cares for us, protects us, and wants the best for us. If you have received Jesus as your Lord and Savior, but you are not experiencing the blessing of God, take heart—He is right there with you. Just like at the gas station that day, God will meet you right where you are and will love you. This is what the rainbow means for us today.

The Abrahamic covenant today seems awfully technical, and for some of us males, it is awfully relevant. What we can truly take from it, though, is that, just as God added grace to Abram's life by changing his name to Abraham and then marked him through the circumcision of the flesh, we have received mercy and grace through Jesus Christ and have been changed into a new creation by the spiritual circumcision of the heart. And like the Hebrew people, we are marked as belonging to God through the New Covenant. The Hebrews were marked physically by physical circumcision, and we are marked by Christ's shed blood. This is what God sees when He looks at you. He is not looking at your sin or your shortcomings; He sees the beauty and perfection of His beautiful and perfect Son. He will never break His promises of love, forgiveness, and blessing toward you because you are in Christ.

Further comparison of the old and new covenants reveals that the Old Covenant is the law, designed to bring judgment. It is designed to bring us to the end of ourselves and to make us realize our need for a savior. The New Covenant, which ushers in that savior, brings instead life, grace, and peace. And it focuses on what Christ has already done. In living in the New Covenant, we can rest in Christ's finished work. The New Covenant is the final covenant because Jesus is *it*. The beginning, the end, the solution, the whole. It is all about him. He is everything we will ever need, and without him there is nothing good. He tells us quite bluntly on the night of his betrayal that we can do *nothing* apart from him, but now we don't have to try because He will never leave us or forsake us, and through him we can do *all things*.[26]

God promises to love us and forgive us through these covenants—and He will—but for us to live fully in Christ and experience all that God has for us in this life, we must seek Him. The scripture in Jeremiah says that God will listen and will be found, but it's conditional upon our seeking and prayer. Interestingly, that day at the gas pump, no one else seemed to notice the majestic rainbow brushed across the sky. People were everywhere—inside the convenience store, at the gas pumps, and driving by in cars. But I seemed to be the only one who noticed the rainbow. I don't point this out to suggest that I was actually the only one who could see it, but that others simply didn't take the time to look, or *to seek*, as the scripture says. They were too distracted by the cares of their world to see the sign of love being sent from their Father.

God never leaves us, but we certainly leave Him. And the only way we can return to Him is to free ourselves from the distractions of this world long enough to hear Him. If we want all that God has to offer, we need to start by offering Him our time and our prayers. It's as simple as that. When we do not

---

[26] Philippians 4:13

take time for Him and keep our mind renewed by His Word, we allow the deceptions of the Enemy to come into our minds and wreak havoc. So, stay in constant communion with your loving Father by walking in the love of Jesus and staying submitted to him through his Word and the Holy Spirit. Put God first—He loves you and has a wonderful plan for your life.

Old Life to New Creation

...if any man be in Christ, he is a new creature: old things are passed away; behold, all things are become new.
2 Corinthians 5:17 KJV

But the Helper, the Holy Spirit, whom the Father will send in my name, he will teach you all things and bring to your remembrance all that I have said to you.
Jesus Christ, John 14:26 ESV

After we are born again, scripture says we are a new entity. We have a new identity in Christ— the spirit is completely renewed, perfected, and holy, then it is sealed with the Holy Spirit and we become a new creation. The very name Christian means *little Christ*, implying that Christ lives in us. He goes wherever we go, and as we are an extension of him; he is primary in and critical to our lives. He can never be asked to stay at church on Sunday or to take a back seat or to be quiet or to be politically correct. These are as absurd as the painting telling the painter to be still and put down the brush. Jesus is ever present and should dominate our thoughts and decision making.

Being a new creation in Christ also means that we find agreement with God. We find out what pleases Him,[27] and He teaches us to agree that those things are for our good. This takes time, though—we must *learn* to agree with Him and His Word, and we must receive guidance from the Holy Spirit.

Without the Holy Spirit the Christian life is quite impossible to live out in victory—and to fulfill all that God has written for you to do. Some never reach this level of maturity in their relationship with God, believing that Jesus died for them to simply have a better life and have the many things they want to do and accomplish. So, they never seek God and find out what He has planned for them, thus never entering into God's plan for their lives. To some degree, this can be blamed on the church and its ministers for preaching against the gifts of the Spirit and the sovereignty of God in error. God is omnipotent and all-knowing, but there are spiritual laws as well as natural to which God holds us, as well as Himself, accountable. He can intervene with miracles, and at the time they are needed they are wonderful, but for a miracle to take place there must be a crisis. Our Father would rather we learn how to cooperate with Him and be partakers of His blessing on our lives, so we have a big part to play in our salvation as well. We cannot do anything without God, but He will not do anything without us. We are

---

[27] Ephesians 5:10

the ones to whom He has given the spiritual authority in this world, and He is waiting for us to take up our identity in Him and begin partnering with Him to build His kingdom, instead of just thinking of ourselves.

Often though, old things remain after our rebirth and new identity in Christ. My salvation story is a prime example. After being reborn, even though I was studying the Word of God with diligence to learn about the salvation I had entered into and ministers had provided valuable information and prayers, there remained significant strife in my home and family. Old unpleasantness stuck around, including arguing and other turmoil-causing behavior. We were so tired and beat down from the past that, frankly, I really wouldn't have minded just going on to heaven. We understood in my home that things were to be made new, so why were they still old? After all, I had accepted the Lord and had prayed and renounced every evil thing not of God, and I was truly seeking God with all my heart. I questioned my pastor on the issue, and I will never forget the image he gave me. He said, "Didn't we pray?" Yes, we had. He said, "Then it is settled in heaven. All that old stuff is gone and done away with and the new life has begun—but you know how sometimes when you have a skunk under your house and you kill it and get it out of there, how sometimes that smell still lingers, and you will still smell it from time to time, but the skunk is dead... it's gone?"

I had never had a skunk under my house, but the analogy was crystal clear: I had entered into a new life with God through Christ and things were certainly different—the skunk was gone—in my spirit I had been renewed and made holy, but in the natural realm there were still going to be flare-ups. I was still going to stink from time to time. I had to accept this reality because I had no other choice. Like anyone, I would have preferred an immediate and automatic transformation of all things old to new, but as long as I had spiritual truths from God to hang onto, then I knew I would be fine... just as long as I knew God was for me, then I could be comforted in believing that things would get better someday.

The next day, armed with the analogy of the skunk but still sad that I had to smell it, my wife and I drove to the grocery store. I grabbed a shopping cart, and we began to walk through the store. As I pushed the cart down the back aisle, my phone rang. It was my stepdad. He and my mother lived 70 miles away, and I hadn't spoken to them for several days (nor had anyone else in my home). After saying hello, my stepdad laughed and said, "Your mother wants to know—how is your skunk doing?"

"Excuse me?"

" Last night, your mother had a dream. In the dream, you were a little boy pushing a grocery basket, and in the grocery basket you had a skunk. So, she wants to know—how is your skunk doing?"

He laughed again at the seemingly outlandish dream my mother had about me. I'm sure he expected the same type of response from me. But I had stopped in my tracks, standing there with one hand on the shopping cart and the other holding the phone, knowing that God himself was conveying a message to me through my stepdad, a message given to my mother in a dream.

So, I confidently said, "Tell her that skunk is dead and gone!"

"Huh? No, you see your mother, she had a dream, and you were ...."

I interrupted, "I know exactly what you said, and I am telling you that skunk is dead and gone."

In the phone call from my stepfather, God was confirming to me that He is for me, that everything really had changed just a few days prior when I called out to Him in truth and was saved. And at that moment He was giving me an opportunity to know it without a doubt and to make my positive confession regarding these things. You can do the same. Not only that—God wants you to! He wants to hear you say out loud that even though you may still stink from time to time, you know that you're a new creation in Christ.

CHAPTER FIVE

CHRIST ALONE OVER THE LAW

Then Moses raised his arm and struck the rock twice with his staff. Water gushed out, and the community and their livestock drank.
Numbers 20:11 NIV

Because you did not trust me enough to demonstrate my holiness to the people of Israel, you will not lead them into the land I am giving them!
God, Numbers 20:12 NLT

Let anyone who is thirsty come to me and drink.
Jesus Christ, John 7:37 NIV

And I myself did not know him, but the one who sent me to baptize with water told me, 'The man on

whom you see the Spirit come down and remain is the
one who will baptize with the Holy Spirit.'
John the Baptist, John 1:33 NIV

I am the way and the truth and the life. No one
comes to the Father except through me.
Jesus Christ, John 14:6 NIV

Knowing that relationship with and submission to Jesus Christ is the answer for experiencing the fullness of God's love and grace here on earth, we must look to Christ himself as he is presented in scripture. Christ is woven throughout all of scripture, but let's look at the story of Moses.

Moses grew up in Egypt during the time that the Israelites were slaves in Egypt, before they entered into their Promised Land. Out of necessity he was abandoned by his Hebrew mother and adopted into Egyptian royalty as a baby. At the age of 40, he killed an Egyptian soldier and ran away to the desert, where God left him for another 40 years before He was ready to use him. (Time apparently needed to get Moses out of Moses.) The job God had for him was to bring the Israelites out of Egypt and into their Promised Land. You've heard most of the story—God sent plagues on Egypt to convince Pharaoh to release the Hebrew slaves, and the Hebrews followed Moses to wander the desert for 40 years, during which time God established many religious processes and procedures among His people, including sending the Ten Commandments down from Mount Sinai. Moses worked hard for the Lord, performing miracles, speaking to the people, leading the people, instructing the people, and following God's commands, but at the end of the road—at 120 years old and at the culmination of God's entire purpose for his life—the Lord did not allow him to enter the Promised Land.

Numbers 20 tells us why God dealt with Moses this way. The Israelites were once again complaining about the food and water they lacked on their journey. God instructed Moses to speak to a rock and bring forth water from it for the people and livestock to drink. Instead, Moses addressed the people in anger, raised his staff, and struck the rock...twice. Water poured out from the rock, and the people and livestock drank. But because Moses did not trust God's instruction to *speak* to the rock, God prevented him from ever seeing the Holy Land, his whole life's purpose.

At first this punishment seemed harsh to me. My relatively unrenewed mind thought, *God knew Moses—he had certainly committed worse sin than disobedience before God ever decided to use him for the deliverance of His people. Yes, I understand that God told him to speak to the rock and he hit it instead, but what about Moses' enormous responsibility of being God's appointed leader for these people, who constantly rebelled, quarreled, and whined, even after seeing God come through for them over and over? People who proved so annoyingly insatiable that at one point, neither Moses nor the Lord seemed to want to claim them?[28] Where's the forgiveness and understanding?*

Regardless how harsh it seems, however, God pronounced this judgment on Moses and made it final. (Later, when Moses would ask Him about going into the Promised Land, the Lord would tell him not to even ask Him about it again[29]). The Lord gave one reason—disobedience—and it was sufficient.

But the reason goes deeper than simple punishment for disobedience. Some 37 years prior to this event, the Israelites led by Moses were at that same location with the same problem—no water. This first time, God instructed Moses to take the staff and *strike* the rock to bring forth water. Moses did, and water came forth.[30] The second time, then, God changed the instruction—Moses was to simply *speak* to the rock for the same result. He did not. Not only did Moses strike it once, he struck it twice, as if to say to God, *I know you did it this way once before, so I know better than you what it takes for water to come out of the rock.*

Moses had no way of knowing, but God's instructions for the water rock pointed to Jesus Christ. His intention was for the first rock strike to be the only rock strike—to foreshadow and symbolize a picture of our Lord Jesus Christ, our Rock, being struck down on Calvary—once, finally, and completely. With His second instruction, God

---

[28] Exodus 32
[29] Deuteronomy 3
[30] Exodus 17

wanted Moses to symbolize another picture, that of a beautiful promise that would come through the Messiah. God told him to simply *speak* to the rock and water would come forth, which is the type of relationship that God knew He would be making available to all people through His Son. Christ was *struck* down for the sin of the entire world, and all we have to do is *speak* to him. Just ask, and the grace that has been provided for all is ours. In speaking to the stricken Lord, we, like the Israelites, receive water—living water—as Jesus said in John 7. That living water is symbolic of the Holy Spirit and His effects in the lives of believers as they conform their thinking to the Word of God.[31]

So, really, when Moses struck the rock for the second time—and twice at that—it was like crucifying Jesus all over again and then eliminating the direct manner with which future Christians would access God. A second crucifixion is not needed and will never happen. Christ's sacrifice was perfect, and when it was accomplished he sat down at the right hand of God the Father. There will never be a need for another sacrifice because that one time is overpayment for any debt we could ever have. And Moses could not have known what future communications with God would look like, but God knew—and He required obedience from Moses to create the picture of it.

While God's punishment for Moses looks harsh and even unwarranted on first glance, it's actually a

---

[31] Galatians 5:22–23, Romans 8:6, 12:2

beautiful example of His grace and love for us. God never intended Moses to lead the children of Israel into the Promised Land because he is representative of the law. Having Moses lead the Hebrew people into the Promised Land sends the message that we, post-resurrection believers, can attain eternal blessing, can get to our promised land on our own, under the law, by self-effort, by good works. We know this to be false (even though many still tend toward "working" our way to heaven. So instead of choosing Moses (the law), God chose Joshua to lead the people in. His name means the same as Jeshua, or Jesus. God wanted to make sure we know that the only way to get across that proverbial "Jordan River" into the promised land of our salvation is a bridge made only of an old rugged cross. No one gets to the Father except through Christ—and Moses' punishment was a critical piece of God telling us that wonderful truth.

CHAPTER SIX

THE SPIRITUAL GARDEN

*Then he told them many things in parables,
saying: "A farmer went out to sow his seed. As he was
scattering the seed, some fell along the path, and the
birds came and ate it up. Some fell on rocky places,
where it did not have much soil. It sprang up quickly,
because the soil was shallow. But when the sun came up,
the plants were scorched, and they withered because
they had no root. Other seed fell among thorns, which
grew up and choked the plants. Still other seed fell on
good soil, where it produced a crop—a hundred, sixty or
thirty times what was sown. Whoever has ears, let them
hear."*
Matthew 13:3–9 NIV

*...A man reaps what he sows. The one who sows to
please his sinful nature, from that nature will reap
destruction; the one who sows to please the Spirit, from*

the Spirit will reap eternal life. Let us not become weary in doing good, for at the proper time we will reap a harvest if we do not give up.
Galatians 6:7-9 NIV

The acts of the flesh are obvious: sexual immorality, impurity and debauchery; idolatry and witchcraft; hatred, discord, jealousy, fits of rage, selfish ambition, dissensions, factions and envy; drunkenness, orgies, and the like. I warn you, as I did before, that those who live like this will not inherit the kingdom of God. But the fruit of the Spirit is love, joy, peace, forbearance, kindness, goodness, faithfulness, gentleness and self-control...
Galatians 5:19–23 NIV

All scripture is God-breathed or given by inspiration of God,[32] and since the Bible often uses the metaphor of a garden to describe the life of faith, it is critical for us as Christ-followers to listen to his teachings and examine our spiritual gardening practices. Without the proper care and attention, our spiritual gardens will not produce healthy growth and prosperity in our lives.

It doesn't take long to identify what has been planted in a garden. If you see tomatoes in a garden, the gardener obviously planted tomato seeds. If you see watermelons, the gardener planted watermelon seeds. If you see cucumbers, the gardener planted cucumber seeds. It's just as easy to identify what has

---

[32] 2 Timothy 3:16, 2 Peter 1:21

been planted and sowed in the heart. In talking with someone, it doesn't take too long before you can tell what sort of seeds they have planted and are sowing in their life—seeds of bitterness, anger, resentment, unforgiveness, or self-pity, perhaps. Or maybe it's obvious that what has been planted are seeds of love, joy, peace, patience, kindness, goodness, faithfulness, gentleness, and self-control. These are all fruit of the Spirit of God, and Jesus died on the cross so you and I could *have* them. What type of seeds are you revealing to others that you've planted and are sowing? The place to get the right seeds is through the Word of God and the fellowship of the Holy Spirit. Without the good seed of God's Word planted in our hearts, we can never find the fullness of His will for our lives, and the fruit of the Spirit will never manifest in our lives. Lesser seed planted and sowed within a heart—seed from the world—produces only corrupted fruit, leading to death in its various manifestations.

God tells us that simply knowing and having the right seed is not enough. It's a good start, certainly, but any farmer will attest to the fact that "seed don't grow in the sack." Imagine a farmer taking this attitude:

I'm not too sure if the weather will be good for farming this year, so I think I'll just hold onto the seed I have, tuck it away in the barn, and play it safe. Who knows—it may not even rain this year! Or it could rain too much! We could have a bad storm, maybe hail! Sometimes armyworms or bollworms get into the crop and kill the whole thing, too. Any of those would ruin the crop and the time I spent planting will have been wasted. It's a smarter plan to save the seed. Plus, this way, I don't have to do any hard work—getting out the old tractor, tilling up the ground, planting the seed, managing the seed, taking care of it.... I know a guy down the road who got a bunch of money from the government not to plant his seed at all. Good incentive—maybe I can get in on that deal. Farming wasn't ever really my strong suit. I'm sure no one will miss the small crop I would produce anyway. Matter of fact, everybody would probably harvest twice as much as me even if I did plant all this seed.

The outcome of this attitude isn't hard to predict—this farmer will not have a harvest, and it's nobody's fault but his. Our lives in Christ are the same. God designed the earth's system of the harvest through sowing and reaping, and He designed the same system in the spiritual realm. Everything we have is in seed form. It might be tangible, such as money, houses, cars, or any other material thing. Or it could be something intangible, like a smile, kindness, or a talent. Perhaps the most important intangible seeds are our words and our time. Everything is a seed, and our lives are largely made up of the choices we make in how and when to sow these seeds.

We shouldn't judge the farmer too harshly—everything he did we do ourselves. If we plant seeds from God by investing ourselves into the things of God, the storms of life could still cause major setbacks. We have dreams, in seed form, that God has placed in our hearts, but it's much easier to simply know that we have the seed stored away than to put in the work of tilling the ground, planting the seeds, and watering God's plans and desires for our lives and those we may affect. Especially because we aren't experts and other Christians are much better at it than we are. And certainly, we have outside influence incentivizing us to leave the seed unplanted—the things of this world always give us reason not to attend to our crop. These reasons are based in sinful fear, covetousness, self-pity, and laziness. God is our provider, and if we will just head in the direction of his plan for our lives He will calm our fears with His providence every time, even if it doesn't look quite how we think it should. And remember, we don't know all we think we do about other people's situations. God does not want us to be in the business of comparing ourselves to others because we lose that battle in our souls every single time. Anytime we begin to complain about the provision or talents God has placed in our lives, we are offending our Creator—this is reason enough not to do it. Finally, laziness only breeds sorrow and often depression over time. Lives of laziness are some of the least fruitful, the least joyful, and the most disappointing.

We must rid ourselves of these excuses because if we don't plant at all, we will not reap a harvest at all. If we don't sow our seeds of love, joy, peace, patience, kindness, goodness, faithfulness, gentleness, and self-control, neither will we reap a harvest of them in our lives. Not planting allows the enemy access into our lives, which can have broad-reaching impacts well beyond our own souls. So, ask the Holy Spirit to till the soil of your heart, plant the seed of God's Word in it, and then begin to give to others all the same wonderful things that God has given you, confidently expecting that your good and loving God will bring an abundant harvest in your life.

Sowing: Thoughts, Words, and Beliefs

Finally, brothers, whatever is true, whatever is honorable, whatever is just, whatever is pure, whatever is lovely, whatever is commendable, if there is any excellence, if there is anything worthy of praise, think about these things.
Philippians 4:8 ESV

...as he thinketh in his heart, so is he...
Proverbs 23:7 KJV

The good person out of the good treasure of his heart produces good, and the evil person out of his evil treasure produces evil, for out of the abundance of the heart his mouth speaks.
Jesus Christ, Luke 6:45 ESV

Death and life are in the power of the tongue: and they that love it shall eat the fruit thereof.
Proverbs 18:21, KJV

Therefore I tell you, whatever you ask in prayer, believe that you have received it, and it will be yours."
Jesus Christ, Mark 11:24 ESV

> *...for we walk by faith, not by sight.*
> *1 Corinthians 5:7 ESV*

> *Grace and peace be multiplied unto you through the*
> *knowledge of God, and of Jesus our Lord, according as*
> *his divine power hath given unto us all things that*
> *pertain unto life and godliness, through the knowledge*
> *of him that hath called us into glory and virtue:*
> *2 Peter 1:2–3 KJV*

In learning about our spiritual gardens, we cannot ignore the importance of *how* we are believing or *what* we are thinking or meditating on. These beliefs and thoughts ultimately manifest in words that are producing a harvest in our lives, either for good or for evil. According to Proverbs 23:7, we are what we think. So what do you think? Are your thoughts honorable, just, pure, lovely, commendable? The opposite? Sometimes one and sometimes the other? Your life will inevitably go the way of your predominant thinking, so it is wise to *decide* to meditate on Godly things. A common response to this charge is that humans can't help what we think, but that is not true. We absolutely can—with the power of the Holy Spirit abiding in us. (And if you want to test your ability, imagine for a day a screen on your forehead projecting all your thoughts for the world to see. You *will* change them.)

Jesus says in the Gospel of Luke that whatever is in our hearts, whether good or evil, will well up and manifest in our words—and it is our words that create and produce either positive or negative results in our lives. If we speak life, love, faith and truth from God's Word, then we will create for God. If we speak bitterness, fear, anger, hatred, and doubt, then we will create for Satan, sowing evil and reaping the consequences.

If your situations and circumstances are terrible and you can't see them being any other way, don't say all the negative you see, or you will continue to have what you say. Say instead the things of God. This doesn't mean that you live a life of denial; it simply means that you refuse to settle for anything short of God's best manifesting in your life. So, if your marriage, finances, health, or anything else is being threatened, speak life into that situation... like this, for example:

I am experiencing some problems right now, but God is greater than anything that can come against me. My God shall supply all my need according to His riches in glory. I am blessed beyond the curse. I am a blessed, redeemed, and loved child of God and His favor surrounds me as a shield. This situation is not how things will be for me; all the promises of God in Christ are yes and amen. My God has granted unto me all things pertaining to this and godliness and the blessing of the Lord is overtaking me. My marriage/my finances/my health are blessed in the name of Jesus Christ!

Finally comes belief. We are called to live by faith, and Jesus promises in an amazing statement that we shall have anything we pray for if we believe we have it when we pray. Obviously, Jesus didn't mean that God would rig the lottery for us or give us somebody else's spouse—those things would be ungodly—but anything that has been provided by grace through the atonement—love, joy, peace, forgiveness, physical and emotional healing, deliverance, financial provision—all these things and more are ours by simply asking and receiving by faith.

But why? What makes us entitled to these things? What gives us the confidence to believe what Jesus said? The new covenant of his precious blood does. When Jesus died on the cross having said, "It is finished,"[33] and then sat down at the right hand of the Father in heaven, he effectively handed over to all believers, who make up the Church, his power and authority to operate in this earthly realm. Jesus was anointed and filled with the Holy Spirit and power, and he went about doing good and healing all who were oppressed of the devil.[34] He completed many miracles and wonderful works while he was here on earth, but now he has given us the task of doing the works he did and even greater works.[35] The key is in believing and being able to see these spiritual truths so vividly in your mind that they become more real to you than the things you can see in the natural realm. The kingdom of God is within you. You are

---

[33] John 19:30
[34] Acts 10:38
[35] John 14:12

Holy-Ghost-powered![36] And His power will work in and through you more when you begin to magnify and esteem spiritual truths more than the natural. When we do this, we will begin to see a greater manifestation of the desired results in the natural realm.

God says that His people are perishing for a lack of knowledge.[37] John Wayne said it this way: "Life is hard; it's harder if you're stupid." You can be uninformed of the truth and not be stupid, but to know the truth, and not act upon it, is stupid. The Lord has made provision for us to avoid negative results, turmoil, stress, strife, depression, sickness, poverty, and much more. He has provided for our complete salvation through Jesus Christ, and now, as stated in 2 Peter, the favor and blessing of God, as well as his peace, can be multiplied in our lives through knowing Jesus and learning more about him—not because God gives us more, but because we learn to partake of and experience through faith the things He has already provided by His grace.

So, claim what is already yours as an empowered, redeemed, victorious, and loved child of the King. Decide to believe His promises for you, and call on the power of the Holy Spirit to change your thoughts and words for the glory of God.

---

[36] Romans 8:10–11
[37] Hosea 4:6

CHAPTER SEVEN

THE MIRACLES OF JESUS

The Gospels of Matthew, Mark, Luke, and John recount many stories of miracles performed by Jesus while he walked the earth. These miracles were intended to reveal the glory of God and, read by us today, can give us insight into what God wants us to know about His power for our lives.

Jesus Adds Super to Your Natural

"Here is a boy with five small barley loaves and two small fish, but how far will they go among so many?" Jesus said, "Have the people sit down." There was plenty of grass in that place, and they sat down (about five thousand men were there). Jesus then took the loaves, gave thanks, and distributed to those who were seated as much as they wanted. He did the same with the fish. When they had all had enough to eat, he said to his disciples, "Gather the pieces that are left

over. Let nothing be wasted." So they gathered them and
filled twelve baskets with the pieces of the five barley
loaves left over by those who had eaten.
John 6:9–13 NIV

Trust in the Lord with all your heart and lean not
on your own understanding; in all your ways submit to
him, and he will make your paths straight.
Proverbs 3:5–6 NIV

Jesus had ministered all day to a crowd of thousands. Toward the end of the day, the disciples came to him with a problem. They were in the middle of nowhere, it was late, and the people of the crowd had not eaten. The disciples wanted Jesus to send the people away so they could go and find food for themselves and their families. Jesus did not honor this request; instead, he did something very strange: he said, "You give them something to eat." The disciples started reasoning. They considered the number of people—about 5,000 men and an unwritten number of women and children—and how much money it would take to feed the crowd—more than half a year's wages for each person to have just one bite of food. Considering their resources, the disciples' conclusion was that Jesus was being unreasonable.

In response, Jesus simply told the disciples to have the people sit down in an orderly manner. He took what provisions they had—five loaves of bread and two fish—looked up to heaven, prayed, and had the disciples begin serving the people from those provisions. When all were served and fulfilled, the leftover food filled 12 baskets—the original five loaves wouldn't have even filled one basket, but *the leftovers from 5,000+ people filled 12.* Just incredible.

The disciples did what we do throughout our lives. They considered the circumstances in front of them and all the natural resources and options and dismissed Christ because his instruction did not fit into their natural reasoning. In this logic, though, they failed to consider Jesus himself. They had with them the one who created them and everything else they could see or touch. Serving as a man, but completely filled with the Holy Spirit, Jesus is not bound by the natural order of things. He recognized the need of the 5,000. He understood the Father's heart and love for the people. He prayed accordingly and served the need. And the Father did not disappoint. He took that small offering and rewarded the people with abundance.

When faced with what seems impossible—like five loaves of bread to feed 5,000 men—and every angle has been analyzed and rendered incapable, turn to God. Shut off your human reasoning, listen to what He is telling you, and take a step in faith because yours is a miracle-working God. Your God is not bound by your natural limitations, so instead of identifying those limits, focus your mental and emotional effort on these holy practices instead:

1. Recognize the need.
2. Seek God through scripture, godly council, and time alone with Him so you can understand His heart concerning the

matter, never forgetting how much He loves you.

3. Pray according to His will, always giving thanks.

4. Start working toward the goal, trusting God to meet you at your point of need. He may not meet your need as you prescribe, but He will indeed meet you.

A final note on this scripture is that once he performed the miracle of feeding the 5,000, Christ immediately retreated to focus on his next assignment. Once our need is met according to God's will, we must set our sights on what He wants next for us. Otherwise, we end up right back where we were before. Once God has grown our faith muscles, He wants us to use them—don't let them go to waste after He has faithfully met your need.

Jesus Wants Us to Be Unafraid

A furious squall came up, and the waves broke over the boat, so that it was nearly swamped. Jesus was in the stern, sleeping on a cushion. The disciples woke him and said to him, "Teacher, don't you care if we drown?"
He got up, rebuked the wind and said to the waves, "Quiet! Be still! "Then the wind died down and it was completely calm. He said to his disciples, "Why are you so afraid? Do you still have no faith?"
Mark 4:37–40 NIV

A strong wind was blowing and the waters grew rough. When they had rowed about three or four miles, they saw Jesus approaching the boat, walking on

> *the water; and they were frightened. But he said to*
> *them, "It is I; don't be afraid."*
> John 6:18–20 NIV

Matthew, Mark, and Luke tell the story of the disciples being in a boat with Jesus when a great storm threatened to sink them. Jesus, was asleep in the back of the boat, causing the disciples to question their teacher's love for them. They woke him and asked if he even cared if they were to drown. Jesus got up, rebuked the wind and the waves, and all was calm. In all three accounts, Jesus then points out the disciples' fear and lack of faith. The disciples assumed that a sleeping Jesus was an uncaring Jesus. They let their natural minds go wild and assumed the worst: that even though Christ's original instruction to them was to "go over to the other side," they would be overcome by the storm and die. They believed that there was nothing to be done, and they believed that their Master did not care.

The story of Jesus walking on water reveals the same condition among the disciples. Christ had sent the disciples in a boat to Bethsaida, and he went to pray. They rowed all night against heavy wind, they were straining at the oars, and they had only made it to the middle of the lake. In a vision, Jesus saw they were in trouble, so he walked to them on the water. When the disciples saw Jesus walking on the water, they thought he was a ghost and were terrified. But Jesus spoke to them and said, "Take courage! It is I. Do not be afraid." He got in the boat and the wind died down. Again, the disciples showed their lack of faith and trust in their Creator and followed their fear instead

Let's learn from the disciples. When we endure terrible storms in this life, or even little squalls, *Christ desires that we don't panic.* Whether the storm is natural, like a hurricane or tornado, or human, like death, addiction, disease, trauma, or abuse, he wants us to remember that we are not alone. And actually, we have a leg up on the disciples here—at that point in time, they were with Jesus in the flesh only and did not have him living inside them by agency of the Holy Spirit. So even though they saw Christ with their own eyes, they ignored his words and forgot his acts. Christ was in one place at one time, but today he lives in each of us. If we are in Christ, the Holy Spirit is in us, teaching us new things, revealing God's will to us, reminding us of things God has said, and causing us to remember the miracles God has performed. So instead of, like the disciples, ignoring what God has said to us through His Word and forgetting what miracles He has performed in our lives and the lives of those around us, we can recognize His constant presence with us. We can quit acting like He is so far away, like He may or may not show up for us, like He may or may not care what happens to us. Instead of magnifying the problems in our life and letting fear take over, we are to magnify the Lord who is right here with us and to remember that He loves us, cares for us, and is faithful.

In the midst of life's storms, start by praising God, thanking Him for what He has already brought

you through and delivered you from. Meditate on
His Word. And remember who Jesus is—your
Friend, your Brother, your Healer, your Provider,
your Redeemer, your King—and speak to him as if he
were sitting right there with you—because he is. He
is willing and able to help in every situation. He loves
you, and no matter how deep you have gotten
yourself into trouble, he wants you to enjoy the
peace that only he can provide. Don't allow fear to
manifest into spoken words of doubt and unbelief.
Because of Jesus' finished work, we have the
authority to speak truth to the storms of life
ourselves, in his name. Be unafraid—Christ is within
you, he loves you, and he will never leave you or
forsake you.

Jesus Sees Past Our Demons

*This man lived in the tombs, and no one could bind
him anymore, not even with a chain. For he had often
been chained hand and foot, but he tore the chains
apart and broke the irons on his feet. No one was strong
enough to subdue him. Night and day among the tombs
and in the hills he would cry out and cut himself with
stones. When he saw Jesus from a distance, he ran and
fell on his knees in front of him. He shouted at the top of
his voice, "What do you want with me, Jesus, Son of the
Most High God? In God's name don't torture me!" For
Jesus had said to him, "Come out of this man, you
impure spirit!" Then Jesus asked him, "What is your
name?" "My name is Legion," he replied, "for we are
many." And he begged Jesus again and again not to
send them out of the area. A large herd of pigs was*

feeding on the nearby hillside. The demons begged Jesus,
"Send us among the pigs; allow us to go into them." He
gave them permission, and the impure spirits came out
and went into the pigs. The herd, about two thousand in
number, rushed down the steep bank into the lake and
were drowned.

Mark 5:3–13 NIV

After calming the fierce storm on the sea, Jesus stepped off the boat and was immediately met by a crazy man living in the tombs—naked, homeless, violent, possessed by demons. He cried out to Jesus, begging him not to torture him. Or rather, *the demons living inside the man compelled him* to cry out—thousands of them (a Legion being somewhere between 3,000 and 6,000). The demons had recognized Jesus as the Son of God, and though they had no part with him as Savior (having given up their home in heaven), they still knew him as their judge. They were terrified of his power.

Jesus, though, was not interested in the demons. He knew the time was coming, certainly, when he would throw Satan and all of his messengers into the abyss,[38] but this was not the time. No, Jesus was after something else. He was after the man. This man who was tormented, destitute, and ragged—Jesus was after *him*. Demon-possessed was not who God had created this man to be, and Jesus intended to set him free. Once Jesus gave the command, the man was freed from demonic oppression. He was so grateful

---

[38] Revelation 9 and 20

that he wanted to follow Jesus, but Christ did not allow it, instead sending him home to tell his loved ones and others in the town what God had done for him.

"Living in the tombs" can mean many things to us—we are tormented by addiction, rejection, anger, poverty, or the tombs of our past—regret or bitterness. If you call a graveyard your home, Christ is nearer than you think. He is approaching the shore of your graveyard home and can free you from these demons. He loves you, and just as he went after the man of the tombs almost 2,000 years ago, he sees past your demons—sees the person God created you to be—and won't stop short of rescuing you from your oppression. Jesus came so that we could live the abundant life we were created for, and setting us free from our torments is how he helps us achieve it. Living the abundant life intended for us means just this—living the life of an overcomer, free from the oppression of demons, free from bitterness, anger, and other baggage weighing us down; living in peace, love, and joy.

Once set free, this peace is not only for us. Just like the man from the tombs, the first thing Christ wants us to do is to share God's goodness and redeeming power. The natural fruit of a real encounter with Jesus is evangelism, an eagerness to share with others the Good News, and your personal experience with the Savior.

Jesus Is Hindered by Unbelief

As Jesus was on his way, the crowds almost crushed him. And a woman was there who had been subject to bleeding for twelve years, but no one could heal her. She came up behind him and touched the edge of his cloak, and immediately her bleeding stopped. "Who touched me?" Jesus asked. When they all denied it, Peter said, "Master, the people are crowding and pressing against you." But Jesus said, "Someone touched me; I know that power has gone out from me." Then the woman, seeing that she could not go unnoticed, came trembling and fell at his feet. In the presence of all the people, she told why she had touched him and how she had been instantly healed. Then he said to her, "Daughter, your faith has healed you. Go in peace."
Luke 8:42–48 NIV

Meanwhile, all the people were wailing and mourning for her. "Stop wailing," Jesus said. "She is not dead but asleep." They laughed at him, knowing that she was dead. [54] But he took her by the hand and said, "My child, get up!" Her spirit returned, and at once she stood up. Then Jesus told them to give her something to eat.
Luke 8:52–55 NIV

But without faith it is impossible to please him: for he that comes to God must believe that he is, and that He is a rewarder of them that diligently seek Him.
Hebrews 11:6 KJ2000

"Be not afraid of their faces: for I am with you to deliver you," says the Lord.

Jeremiah 1:8 KJ2000

A man named Jairus came to Jesus and asked him to come to his house. He was distraught because his 12-year-old daughter was sick and dying. Jesus went with him, and on the way felt someone touch him so that power went out of him for healing. The person who touched him was a woman who had been suffering for 12 years with an issue of blood, having been to many doctors who couldn't heal her. She had heard about Jesus and knew that he could heal her if she could just touch even the edge of his garment. So in her unclean state, disallowed by law from being in public or from touching anyone, the woman risked punishment of death to get to the One she knew could make her well. Upon being touched, Jesus felt power leave his body and sought the source of this simple touch of faith. The woman came forth and was completely healed of her long-term illness.

After healing this woman Jesus continued to Jairus' home, and on the way, a messenger brought the news that his daughter had died, which didn't faze Jesus. He continued on to the house, telling the broken father, "Don't be afraid, just believe, and she will be healed." When they arrived, many people were at the home wailing and playing flutes (according to their mourning custom), and Jesus told them to stop because the girl was, in fact, not dead, but only sleeping. Knowing full well she was dead, the people laughed at him. Jesus put them all outside except Peter, James, John, and the girl's parents. He grabbed the girl by the hand and told her to get up.

Her spirit reentered her body, and she got up and ate.

These two stories, woven together as one, reveal something important about faith and unbelief. These two powers act as if in a game of tug-o-war, where one side pulls the other until one finally wins out, defeating the other. We often go back and forth between faith and unbelief in our hearts and minds, not knowing that God's power working in our lives depends on which wins out. Faith can move mountains, but unbelief can hinder the manifestation of the answered prayer. This is why Christ rewarded the bleeding woman's faith alone, and it is why he cast the nonbelievers out of Jairus' home. The woman's doctors and community had pronounced her unclean and ill forever, but Christ ignored this unbelief and looked instead upon her faith for healing. The mourners at Jairus' home all thought that Jesus was too late; they knew that once something is dead, it is dead, without any chance of life again, so Jesus ejected them and left only believers in the room. Recognizing that unbelief would be a hindrance to raising the dead, he only allowed those whose hope would allow faith to conquer their doubt and unbelief.

If something seems dead, without hope of resurrection—a relationship, a career, a plan, a ministry, a home, a body plagued by illness—know first that God is not moved by time or appearance. It does not matter what the situation looks like or what anyone says about it. God has the final say and can make the dead alive. He even tells us this through the disciples mentioned in this passage—Peter, James, and John, in that order, were allowed to stay in the room where the girl would be raised from the dead. The name Peter means *stone*, James means *to supplant*, and John means *God is gracious*. The Holy Spirit, author of the Bible, blessed us with some hidden manna through typology by mentioning those disciples in that order—he wants to show us that through Jesus Christ, the law (*stone*) was replaced (*supplanted*) by grace (*God is gracious*). And if Christ has the power to supplant the law and save us by grace, he has the power to resurrect anything in our lives that is dead or dying.

Second, work to eliminate unbelief, knowing that Christ considers it a hindrance to working miracles. We may find it easy to say that God can do anything, but we have trouble actually believing that He will do it for *us* or that He will do it in *this* situation. Look again at the bleeding woman. She had every reason not to seek Christ for healing her sickness. She had been pronounced eternally sick and could have believed that. She had been taken out of society and could have accepted that. She chose to believe the power of God instead, and it paid off. The same opportunity is available for you and me today. We can look at all the negativity, death, and illness we have been told of—by a counselor, doctor, financial advisor, or anyone else who said we wouldn't make it—and hinder the possibility for healing. Or we can look at our God, speak faith-filled words based upon the knowledge that He still performs miracles today, and make room for Him to do it.

In eliminating unbelief, we will certainly run into fear of judgment from others, even from those with whom we are closest. Both Jairus and the bleeding woman from the scriptures faced this issue, and we will too. Given pressure from the mourners, Jairus could easily have joined them and written off the life-raising power of Christ. Given pressure from the crowd, the bleeding woman could have caved to the fear of being called "unclean" or "crazy." Because we live in the world with crowds of people, we understand well this fear. Any hesitation to lean on God comes from fear of human judgment, and it must be eradicated, for we are told in Hebrews that we cannot please God without faith. This should be far scarier than being judged by man. God Himself spoke of this in Jeremiah, essentially telling him not to fear what people think. One thing we can be sure of— if God tells us not to be afraid of something, He will surely protect us from it. So make the decision to believe God without worrying about what others think. This type of faith pleases Him immensely.

Jesus Honors Our Prayers for Others

A few days later, when Jesus again entered Capernaum, the people heard that he had come home. They gathered in such large numbers that there was no room left, not even outside the door, and he preached the word to them. Some men came, bringing to him a paralyzed man, carried by four of them. Since they could not get him to Jesus because of the crowd,

they made an opening in the roof above Jesus by digging
through it and then lowered the mat the man was lying
on. When Jesus saw their faith, he said to the paralyzed
man, "Son, your sins are forgiven."
Mark 2:1–12 NIV

Once again teaching to a large crowd, Jesus was presented with a paralytic to heal—but in an uncommon manner. Because the crowd was so large and they could not even get in the door to see Jesus, friends of the paralytic man dug a hole in the roof and lowered him through it. All three accounts of this event say the same thing: Jesus saw the faith *of the friends*, and the paralytic was healed. It wasn't the faith of the paralytic that blessed Jesus; it was the faith of his friends. And the Lord's response was one of love, salvation, and healing for their friend.

This story is enormously encouraging for believers. It tells us that we can have a profound effect on the lives of others. Whom are you believing for? Is it an unsaved loved one, a sick friend, a rebellious child, or a spouse that has withdrawn from you emotionally? Don't stop believing that God has a plan of salvation, deliverance, and healing for that very person. He sees your faith, and He is honored and glorified in your caring for another. Jesus is blessed when you share your faith with them and when you pray for them.

Others' situations can seem impossible, and we can fall prey to the belief that it's not our problem. Sometimes, when we are close to the manifestation of the miracles we are believing for, we give up for either of these reasons. Angels weep on these occasions because they are unable to carry out their instructions to deliver blessings to God's children because we turn off our faith, like shutting off a water faucet when the life-giving water is on its way through. If the paralytic's friends had given up because it was too difficult or because they weren't personally paralyzed, Jesus wouldn't have had the opportunity to perform healing at all. God has poured out a super-abundance of grace through His precious Son Jesus Christ. Receive it by faith for someone you love today. And know that what you make happen for others God will make happen for you.

CHAPTER EIGHT

GOD'S TRANSCENDING PEACE—FOR US

Peace I leave with you, my peace I give to you; not as the world gives do I give to you. Let not your heart be troubled, neither let it be afraid.
Jesus Christ, John 14:27 NKJV

I have told you these things, so that in me you may have peace. In this world you will have trouble. But take heart! I have overcome the world.
Jesus Christ, John 16:33 NIV

Be anxious for nothing, but in everything by prayer and supplication, with thanksgiving, let your requests be made known to God; and the peace of God, which surpasses all understanding, will guard your hearts and minds through Christ Jesus.
Philippians 4:6–7 NKJV

For our struggle is not against flesh and blood, but against the rulers, against the authorities, against the powers of this dark world and against the spiritual forces of evil in the heavenly realms.
Ephesians 6:12 NIV

After what I consider to be my real salvation and God calling me to ministry, my family struggled with finances. I have seen extremes in this area of my life—times where I've had much and times where I've had nothing or very little. And this happened to be a time of severe lack. Pretending with God had ended, and I was being trained up to be made useful in my calling; we had changed everything in our lives and were living for the Lord. For several years, I spent 16 to 18 hours a day either in the Word, in prayer, or in church. We closed every business we owned and suffered total losses on some of them: a bar, a home improvement company, a car lot, stock market investments, and bad real estate deals. At the car lot, we had sold cars to many people on credit, an endeavor that ended in disaster for not having placed any kind of tracking devices on the vehicles. Nobody paid for the cars, the car lot office was destroyed by a hurricane, and we still held dozens of car titles with nothing to show for them. We down-sized by moving into one of our rental properties, and our personal new cars, trucks, and motorcycles had to be sold. We began driving far less dependable cars, and we faced the chance of losing even the smaller home we had moved into. It was hard not to be bitter. And the stress was enormous.

As He often has in critical times, the Lord gave me a dream. I saw myself at a park where I used to walk my dog, Brutus. It is a great park, with a creek running through it and trails cutting through the tall pine forest. Brutus loved going to that park. Sometimes my wife, Tovana, would come along, making it even more special for me. There is a historic marker in the park where Sam Houston camped his army alongside the creek at a settlers' farm on his way to San Jacinto, not far from there, where he defeated Santa Anna and the Mexican Army to gain Texas' independence. The day in the dream was very peaceful and beautiful, with the breeze blowing through the pines. I looked up to the top of the trees toward the sky, which was blue and bright. The trees all reached up into the sky, as I had seen many times, but this time they seemed more alive— it was as if they were truly giving praise to God and reaching toward the heavens. And on the tops of the trees all across the forest I saw cars being held up to the heavens as if being given as an offering to God. It was bizarre, but very real to me. I knew what the positioning of the cars meant, but I didn't want to believe it. To my right were two men, whom I somehow knew to be angels, sitting on a park bench. Pointing toward the cars elevated above the tree-tops, I asked one of the men, "Is this God?" In other words, I wanted to know if what I was seeing was a message from God or if it was just some crazy mix-up in my emotions. One of the men looked me straight in the eyes and said very matter-of-factly, "Yes." I gazed at the beauty of this simple gesture, somehow feeling overwhelmed that God had gone to the trouble of showing me the way.

I woke up with understanding of what I had to do. I explained it to Tovana, and as is the Lord's gracious custom with spouses seeking His will, He confirmed it to us by giving us *peace*. It was approaching Christmastime, and I sat down and composed a letter to all of the people who owed us money for the cars. It simply told them that Tovana and I had come to know the Lord and had experienced His wonderful love and forgiveness. We included signed car titles in the letters as a gift that Christmas in an expression of love and forgiveness, just as we had received from God. We mailed them out that day, and, even though we hadn't been able to find these people in the past, none of the letters or car titles ever came back as undeliverable.

It was a true blessing for us to be able to give away all of those cars. We put God first in that financial situation and were given peace. And after several years, Tovana and I were once again driving new vehicles, safer in our financial situation only for trusting God alone. We have learned how to cooperate with God's principle of sowing and reaping, of forgiveness, and of living a life of faith expressed through love. It is a wonderful, peaceful place.

We deal with hard things in this life while we're here—and no one is exempt. Part of living the abundant life Christ describes for us is not that these things go away, but that we have peace while we go through them. On the last night Jesus spent with his disciples, he had many things to share with them. He gave them instructions about the New Covenant and explained about the Holy Spirit and eternal life. He warned them of many bad things that would come because they had been chosen by him. He gave them authority to use his name. He prayed for them. And in a very personal, beautiful act, he gave them his peace—the same peace that allowed Jesus to sleep in the midst of the storm, to speak to his creation and tell it to be still, to walk untouched through the midst of those trying to throw him off a cliff, to never be carnal, to always forgive, to always love, and to always be in communion with the Father—this peace now belonged to the disciples and belongs to us.

When we struggle to be at peace, Jesus is the only answer. He, very simply, has provided for your peace. In the midst of the storms of life, no matter who or what is coming against you, Jesus will calm your heart and mind. Through the cross, through the unlimited access we now have to the Father, we can receive the peace of God, a peace that goes unmatched by anything offered by this world. Note, though, that the scriptures do not say God will always take away what pains us. But the promise is He will give us His peace while we endure it.

To learn to look to Christ in times of strife, first we must understand where our lack of peace comes from. Before I knew the Lord, when I was enduring tough circumstances, my natural response was to turn against people, to be bitter and angry at who had hurt me, who had wronged me, and to seek retribution through the world's channels. The truth, though, is that the real battle is in the unseen, spiritual realm. Magnifying my problems through a worldly lens actually gave the Enemy more authority to operate in my life. But when I chose to pray instead, asking the Lord what to do, He powerfully said, "Stay close to me; they are afraid of me." In a time when I thought that God had gone away because of the fear and failure I was experiencing, He had actually never left me at all—my awareness of His presence had slipped as I focused on the works of the Enemy coming against me. As I refocused on Jesus and allowed the Holy Spirit to bring me into an awareness of his presence, the Enemy began to flee in terror of the King. The things that caused me stress did not always go away—I just learned to walk through them with God's peace.

Next, we must look to what scripture—what God—says about trials. There are many, but the following is full of promises straight from God regarding worry:

> *Then Jesus said to his disciples: "Therefore I tell you, do not worry about your life, what you will eat; or about your body, what you will wear. Life is more than food, and the body more than clothes. Consider the ravens: They do not sow or reap, they have no storeroom or barn; yet God feeds them. And how much more valuable you are than birds! Who of you by worrying can add a single hour to his life? Since you cannot do this very little thing, why do you worry about the rest?*

*Consider how the lilies grow. They do not labor or spin.
Yet I tell you, not even Solomon in all his splendor was
dressed like one of these. If that is how God clothes the
grass of the field, which is here today, and tomorrow is
thrown into the fire, how much more will he clothe you,
O you of little faith! And do not set your heart on what
you will eat or drink; do not worry about it. For the
pagan world runs after all such things, and your Father
knows that you need them. But seek his kingdom, and
these things will be given to you as well. Do not be
afraid, little flock, for your Father has been pleased to
give you the kingdom."*
Luke 12:22–32

This passage reveals the simplest, most powerful
piece of our relationship with God the Father, God
the Son, and God the Spirit—He loves us
unconditionally and unrelentingly. Never for a
second allow any trial, stressor, evil, worry, fear, or
pain to give rise to the thought that He doesn't. That
is a bold lie of the Enemy that should be
unacceptable to us. In the scripture, Jesus points out
how God takes care of His creatures—ravens, lilies,
and grass—all of which He considers less than His
human creation. So logic follows, then, that He will
take care of us even more. Christ also uses the image
of Solomon to drive the point harder. Solomon was
perhaps the greatest of all the natural kings of Israel.
God blessed him enormously with wealth, power,
and status, and his kingdom showed it. And yet,
Christ says that the lilies of the field are dressed
better than Solomon ever was—urging us to

understand just how much *more* God will provide for us than the lilies. What we see as simple earthly plants are actually dressed in majestic splendor, more so even than King Solomon was, and God will provide for us even more than that. In all things, our Father will take care of us. And because He loves us so much, He does not want us to waste our time on worry. Your Heavenly Father is not worried. Cast your care upon Him every day so that you are not hindered in glorifying Him on earth.

Finally, like the disciples did, use the authority Christ has given you to speak to the mountains in your life:

Spirit of poverty, strife, rejection, fear, sickness, depression, bitterness, hatred...Jesus warned me that you would come, but you cannot stay. Jesus has already defeated you, and right now, in the name of Jesus, I command you to go and not return.

Believe that it is done, and begin to praise your God who cannot lie. Call upon the gift of peace given to you by your loving Savior. Allow it to dominate you, and practice focusing on *that presence* instead of on the presence of evil. Mediate on it, and fill your mind with promises God has made to you in His Word. Through these acts, you will become strong— not because you are strong, but because your God is. Jesus loves you, and he is interceding for you even now in the face of whatever your trials may be.

CHAPTER NINE

THE GIFT OF FREE WILL

Paths to the pastorate are often not straightforward—my own has certainly included many curves and steep hills. I was ordained three times and, after a few years as a pastor, I had served under several different ministries. I preached at several churches and did some prison ministry, street ministry, nursing home ministry, and such. One ministry, a new church, had even given me an office with *Pastor Will* on the door. God had called me away from all of them, though, and there were churches on every corner and preachers on many of the TV channels. I formed another ministry, and my wife was one of my few encouragers. I honestly felt, though, that even she, if I suggested it, would have no problem with me just shelving the whole idea of being a pastor.

Being trained in the Word by God through full emersion though, I had burning inside of me the things He was teaching me. I longed to share them with the world. I knew that God had done great things for me and had put an overwhelming desire in me to preach and teach His Word. And it seemed like everywhere I went, men and women of God passed on encouragement from Him regarding the gifts of ministry they saw in me. Many prophecies had been spoken over me regarding my ministry, but I was getting discouraged. It seemed as if no one wanted to hear what I had to say, and I wondered why God needed *me*.[39] I prayed, asking God to tell me if I was really supposed to be a preacher. Then I waited for His response, having learned that when a child of God prays earnestly requesting truth and direction—and seriously waits for and expects an answer—an answer surely comes.

Once again, God sent me the answer in a dream. I was in a familiar courtyard of some apartments where my mother and I had lived in Texas City, Texas when I was a boy. I knew it well. I was walking across the courtyard and turned to my right to see

---

[39] It is my belief that unless called by God to do so, no one should ever enter the ministry. Otherwise, they will be working with only their own strength. Their ministry will not be blessed, and they can potentially harm God's children. And some ministers called by God to the five-fold ministry are not called to the position they are in, many being relegated to administrative and other work hindering their anointing.

Jesus walking with me. I felt happy. There was a crowd of people standing across the grass about 25 feet away. The people looked at me with desperate longing; their faces told me they needed direction and guidance—as if they were saying, *what about us?* I felt compassion toward them, the compassion of Jesus the Shepherd for His sheep. I looked to the Lord as if to ask Him, *what about them?* He faced straight ahead, silent. He didn't say anything, but He didn't have to. He didn't answer me directly, but I understood His meaning in an instant. If I didn't fulfill my calling—if I didn't preach the Gospel and help these people and others by leading them into His truth, then they would not be coming with us. They wouldn't hear the Good News or be saved. They wouldn't be discipled or grow in relationship with Him. And they wouldn't disciple others.

God's answer to me could not be a simple *yes* or *no* because God has given us free will. We have a choice in everything we do because our motives are of the utmost importance to God. He wants us to choose Him out of love and gratitude instead of by compulsion. This critical piece of our faith enables God to be glorified—if He were to force His children to love and follow Him, there would be no miracles, no transformation, no sacrifice, no passion for Christ, no reason for us to go deeper in relationship with our Father. Given free will, if we say *no* to God's call, He still loves us, but we forfeit the plans He has written for us. We don't carry out His purposes by choosing something else—by choosing a life seriously lacking in peace, joy, and fulfillment.

Even though my ministry had been rocky, my choice was easy. In fact, there was no choice. God told me that I am a minister of the Gospel of Jesus Christ, and the compassion of Jesus lives inside me to help me love his people, teach them, and shepherd them to be with him for all eternity.

Examine your free will... examine your heart. What is the plan God has for you that you have yet to choose? What doubt and unbelief is stopping you? Are you allowing the enemy a place to fortify in your heart? Ask God to remove your doubt, your unbelief, and the Enemy's hold on you—and reveal to you His way. Living within God's plan, walking in close relationship with Him daily, and submitting to His lordship is the only way to receive fulfillment and joy in this life. And whatever God is leading you to do, do it with your whole heart.

CHAPTER TEN

DO IT NOW

Since 2009, God has been showing me the numbers 911. I can count on looking at the clock at 9:11. I see 911 on documents, addresses, license plates, all sorts of places. He has it ever before me. One example happened recently on the day we set our clocks back for Daylight Savings. I intended to be at the church by 10:00 a.m., so after getting ready, I looked at the only clock I knew would be right in the house—my phone, which automatically adjusts the time. When I picked it up, it was, of course, 9:11 a.m. I went downstairs to the kitchen, where I saw an invitation on the counter for my daughter's baby shower, which would be held at the address 911. This type of experience has become my normal. When it first began, it scared me a little. I didn't know if the Lord was telling me there was going to be another terrible tragedy or catastrophe on this date. I studied all of the 911 scriptures to see if anything would be quickened in my spirit to make me know what God was trying to teach me. I learned a lot, but nothing that seemed relevant. After praying, I gained peace and understanding. The Lord is trying not to scare me, but to prepare me. He is simply letting me feel His since of urgency regarding the work we have to do for Him—for the church, for the Kingdom, to prepare hearts and minds for His impending return.

I have long thought of land as the most valuable natural asset. Many people say gold and silver, but to me land is special. More gold and silver can be mined from the ground, but they aren't making any more land, and the population of the world is ever increasing. The same goes for time in the spiritual realm. God is providing more of it, in the sense that as long as we have tomorrows, there will be more time. The problem is we are not guaranteed tomorrow. God says that *this* is the day of your salvation, and we should be busy doing His work in the world. Every day that passes is a day you can't get back. Yesterday really did end last night, and the only thing left of the time you were given yesterday is God's record of how you spent it. One day we will give account of our time and every idle word before God.

This is not a dress rehearsal, and we should be about the Lord's business. We need to make our lives about these things: first, receiving God's free gift of salvation through Jesus Christ; next, learning to experience the fullness of the new identity in Christ, never letting memories be bigger than dreams, seeing only God's provision instead of our lack, living in God's strength all the days of the life provided and accomplishing all the wonderful things He has in store; and finally, sharing our testimony with others to the glory of God. I hope to hear yours one day.

A little while ago I finished making what I hope to be my final changes to this manuscript. I closed my laptop and sat quietly for a bit thinking of the Lord and being thankful for his goodness. Then I picked up my phone to see if I had missed any calls, ready to move into the next thing He has for me to do... the time was 9:11 p.m.

Made in the USA
Columbia, SC
03 June 2019